# ASTRONAUT TRAVEL GUIDES

# THE SUN

## NICK HUNTER

Raintree

**www.raintreepublishers.co.uk**
Visit our website to find out
more information about
Raintree books.

**To order:**
☎ Phone 0845 6044371
🖷 Fax +44 (0) 1865 312263
🖳 Email myorders@raintreepublishers.co.uk

Customers from outside the UK please telephone +44 1865 312262

Raintree is an imprint of Capstone Global Library
Limited, a company incorporated in England and
Wales having its registered office at 7 Pilgrim
Street, London, EC4V 6LB – Registered company
number: 6695582

Edited by Nancy Dickmann and Laura Knowles
Designed by Steve Mead
Original illustrations © Capstone Global
    Library Ltd 2013
Picture research by Mica Brancic
Originated by Capstone Global Library Ltd
Printed and bound in China by CTPS

ISBN 978 1 406 23978 2 (hardback)
16 15 14 13 12
10 9 8 7 6 5 4 3 2 1

ISBN 978 1 406 23988 1 (paperback)
17 16 15 14 13
10 9 8 7 6 5 4 3 2 1

**British Library Cataloguing in Publication Data**
Hunter, Nick.
The Sun. – (Astronaut travel guides)
523.7-dc23
A full catalogue record for this book is available
from the British Library.

**Acknowledgements**
We would like to thank the following for
permission to reproduce photographs: ESA
pp. 5 top and 10 (S. Corvaja, 2011), 17 (ESA/
SOHO); Getty Images p. 14 (The Bridgeman Art
Library/Harrogate Museums and Art Gallery,
North Yorkshire, UK); Grace Wolf-Chase p. 34;
Library of Congress p. 31 bottom; NASA pp. 4
(Bill Ingalls), 5 middle and 19 (SOHO (ESA &
NASA)), 5 bottom and 31 top (Johnson Space
Center), 7 (Phil Jones), 9 (JPL-Caltech/R. Hurt
(SSC)), 20 (SOHO (ESA & NASA)), 25 (Visible
Earth/EOS Project Science Office/Goddard
Space Flight Center.), 26 (Goddard Space Flight
Center), 37; Science Photo Library pp. 15 (Royal
Astronomical Society), 18 (HR Bramaz, ISM),
23 (US Department of Energy), 28 (Detlev Van
Ravenswaay), 33 (Babak Tafreshi); Shutterstock
pp. 6 (© Richard Williamson), 12 (© George
Bailey), 27 (James Thew), 39 (© Andriano), 40-41
(© Martiin/Fluidworkshop).

Design image elements reproduced with
permission of Shutterstock/© Argus/© Igor
Zh./© Reistlin Magere.

Cover photograph of a Sun plume reproduced
with permission of NASA.

We would like to thank Dr Grace Wolf-Chase,
Paolo Nespoli, and ESA for their invaluable help
in the preparation of this book.

Every effort has been made to contact copyright
holders of material reproduced in this book.
Any omissions will be rectified in subsequent
printings if notice is given to the publisher.

# CONTENTS

Some words are shown in bold, **like this**. You can find out what they mean by looking in the glossary.

## DON'T FORGET

These boxes will remind you what you need to take with you on your big adventure.

## NUMBER CRUNCHING

Don't miss these little chunks of data as you whizz through the travel guide!

## AMAZING FACTS

You need to know these fascinating facts to get the most out of your space safari!

## WHO'S WHO?

Find out about the space explorers who have studied the Universe in the past and today.

# FASTEN YOUR SEATBELT!

Nowadays we can travel anywhere we choose on planet Earth. However, there are only about 500 people who have ever left Earth, and only 12 people have landed on the Moon.

What would it take to travel beyond the Moon to the planets Venus and Mars, or even to the Sun – the star at the centre of our **solar system**? Spacecraft have been built that have travelled millions of kilometres to the edges of our solar system, but these spacecraft have not carried humans up till now.

Rockets are used to launch unmanned spacecraft into outer space. These spacecraft give us images and data about the Sun, planets, and the stars.

### ROCKET POWER

The first thing you will need to travel into space is a powerful rocket. The force of **gravity** pulls us all towards Earth. To escape Earth's gravity, spacecraft need to reach speeds of 40,300 kilometres (25,000 miles) per hour. This means they need to carry a huge quantity of fuel. Being launched into space is a bit like travelling in a huge bomb or firework.

### STAYING ALIVE

Earth and its **atmosphere** provide everything we need to stay alive. If you're travelling in space, you'll need to take all these things with you. For example, without **oxygen** to breathe you wouldn't survive longer than a few minutes.

Meet astronaut Paolo Nespoli on page 10.

Turn to pages 20–21 to discover more about the surface of the Sun.

Find good crewmates for your dangerous journey on pages 30–31.

## DON'T FORGET

- Take a spacesuit with a helmet to keep you alive, especially if you're planning to leave the spacecraft
- Exercise equipment will help you keep healthy while you're cooped up in a spacecraft
- Bring a camera to take some great photos to show your friends when you get back!

# JOURNEY TO THE SUN

People love to travel to warmer countries. But if you tried to travel to the Sun itself, you would get more than you bargained for.

## HOW LONG WOULD IT TAKE?

The fastest speed ever recorded by a human-made object was the *Helios* **probe** that **orbited** the Sun in the 1970s. The probe travelled at about 240,000 kilometres (150,000 miles) per hour. At these amazing speeds, a spacecraft would take just under one month to reach the Sun, which is 150 million kilometres (93 million miles) from Earth. However, at current speeds for **crewed** space flight, the journey would last around six months.

There are about 2,000 stars visible to the human eye.

## ON THE WAY

There are two planets between Earth and the Sun. Both Venus and Mercury are incredibly hot. Venus's atmosphere is filled with clouds of acid that would destroy your spacecraft. Mercury has no atmosphere, meaning that it has no protection from the Sun's **energy**.

It will be even hotter closer to the Sun. In 2015, a space probe will be launched to travel closer to the Sun than ever before. It will orbit the Sun around 6 million kilometres (just under 4 million miles) above its surface. The probe will have to withstand temperatures that would melt metals such as aluminium, and would be far too hot for any living things to stand.

## NUMBER CRUNCHING

The Sun is 150 million km (93 million miles) from Earth. Travelling to the Sun would be roughly the same distance as travelling around the equator almost 4,000 times.

Mercury is the closest planet to the Sun. Here you can see it passing in front of the Sun.

Mercury

## THE BASICS

The Sun measures 1,392,000 kilometres (866,000 miles) in **diameter**. Earth would fit inside the Sun about one million times. The Sun sits at the centre of our solar system. Eight planets travel in orbit around it from the nearest planet, Mercury, to faraway Neptune. The Sun is also orbited by various lumps of rock or metal called asteroids or comets, some of which are big enough to qualify as **dwarf planets**.

## NUMBER CRUNCHING

The Sun has been shining for about 5 billion years – but don't worry, it's not going anywhere! The Sun is about halfway through its lifetime, so should shine for another 5 billion years.

## AN ATTRACTIVE DESTINATION

The planets are held in orbit around the Sun by the force of gravity. In the same way, the Moon and various human-made **satellites** go around the Earth because of gravity. Gravity holds the Universe together, attracting all objects towards each other. We only really notice the force when it is exerted by massive objects like planets and stars. As you get closer to the Sun, you need to be careful and not slow down, otherwise its gravity will pull you in.

Although the Sun is huge compared to Earth and bigger than many other stars, it is not one of the biggest or brightest stars in our galaxy. The Sun is big enough to give out huge amounts of energy, which gives us the light and heat that keeps everything alive on Earth. The Sun is mostly made of **hydrogen gas**, which is the fuel that generates all its energy.

The Sun is much bigger than Earth, so its gravity is much stronger.
Here, you can see how tiny Earth is compared to the Sun.
However, they are really much further apart.

# INTERVIEW WITH AN ASTRONAUT

Paolo Nespoli is an Italian astronaut with the European Space Agency (ESA). In 2007, Paolo went into space for 15 days, and in 2010 he spent a further 6 months in space. In total, he has orbited Earth an amazing 2,782 times.

**Q** *Your very first trip into space was on a space shuttle. What did it feel like on take-off? What were you thinking?*

**A** Going up in space is a risky business in a certain way, because you are strapped to a car that is going up in space propelled almost by an atomic explosion … And on top of that you have to add the fact that you don't just go up for a fun ride – you go up to accomplish something, to accomplish some goals which are technically challenging and complex.

So what I actually felt was, on one side, some kind of happiness that the long wait and the long training was finished, this was the real thing. On the other side, I felt a little bit of apprehension. Would I perform properly as I was requested to? Would everything be okay … or would I make a mistake about something? But everything went pretty good. You go up and nothing happens, you just enjoy the ride. It is quite an amazing feeling.

**Q When you came back from the International Space Station, was it difficult to get used to not being weightless?**

**A** My first ride, which was considered a short duration flight, was 15 days. Coming back, I really felt the effects of gravity pretty heavily, and so I was just wondering how I'm going to feel when I come back after six months, and now I know it's pretty bad.

I felt I weighed, I don't know, two or three hundred kilograms. Just lifting my arm was something that I needed to do consciously and pay attention to. I mean, I had a watch on and I felt the watch was weighing three kilos on my arm. Walking was very difficult, both because of the muscles … but also because of nausea, balance problems, all sorts of things like that.

**Q If you could travel anywhere in the Universe, where would you like to go, and what would you hope to find?**

**A** I would look for a planet somewhere that has more or less the same characteristics of Earth … I really believe that we are not alone in the universe. I mean, if you look at the amount of stars, or planets – we are talking about millions, if not billions of planets – it's impossible, in my opinion, that there are not planets that are similar to Earth. So, I would be curious to go farther away and discovering an Earth-like planet somewhere.

# DISCOVERING THE SUN

Sometime between 5,000 and 3,500 years ago, Stonehenge was built on Salisbury Plain in southern England. No one is sure why it was built. What we do know is that, on the longest day of each year, the Sun rises and shines directly through the gateway of the structure.

Was Stonehenge a temple, a calendar, or a combination of the two?

## ANCIENT KNOWLEDGE

Stonehenge shows that people have studied and worshipped the Sun and its movements since the earliest times. The study of stars and planets is called astronomy. Ancient people knew that the Sun gave them heat and light to live their lives and grow their crops. The path of the Sun across the sky told them the time of day and the season of the year.

Although ancient people knew the importance of the Sun, they knew little about it. They did not understand that Earth's journey around the Sun was the driving force behind our years and seasons. Nor did they know how the Sun produced so much energy. Ancient people thought the Sun orbited Earth.

## AMAZING FACTS

The ancient Egyptians believed the Sun was pushed across the sky by a giant scarab beetle! The idea came from scarab beetles' habit of pushing around a ball of dung containing their eggs.

## COPERNICUS' BREAKTHROUGH

It was not until 1543 that Polish astronomer Nicolaus Copernicus published his theory that Earth and all the other planets orbit the Sun. He also explained how Earth's orbit around the Sun controls the seasons.

## CONTROVERSIAL THEORY

In 1609, Galileo Galilei made one of the first **telescopes**. His observations of the Sun and planets supported Copernicus' theories. This got him into trouble with the Catholic Church, who said the theory was against their teaching.

Astronomers such as Galileo studied the movements of the Sun and planets out of more than just curiosity. Accurate information on these movements was essential to help ships **navigate** their way around the world.

Galileo's work was the start of a period called the Scientific Revolution. Many discoveries were made that form the basis of modern science. Knowledge of the Sun was increasing all the time. In the late 1600s, Gian Domenico Cassini calculated the distance to the Sun and Sir Isaac Newton explained how the Sun's force of gravity held planets in orbit around it.

## STUDYING THE SURFACE

Over the centuries, astronomers were able to find out more about the features on the surface of the Sun, such as **sunspots** and **solar flares**. In the 1800s, new photographic techniques made it easier to study the Sun. Astronomers also made discoveries about what the star was made of.

Studying the Sun can be very dangerous, even from Earth! If you look directly at the Sun through a telescope without protecting your eyes, the intense glare will cause blindness. Special equipment had to be invented to study the Sun, including huge telescopes and instruments that can take detailed images of the star's surface.

## DON'T FORGET

You'll want to study the Sun on your trip. Here are some things that will help you:

- A dark filter that will enable you to look at the Sun without damaging your eyes
- Instruments to measure the Sun's invisible but highly dangerous **radiation**
- Equipment to track the waves below the surface of the Sun that tell us more about how the star works.

## THE SPACE AGE

Until the 1960s, all astronomers had to view the Sun through Earth's atmosphere. Astronomers had to hope there were no clouds between them and the Sun. However, space travel meant astronomers could now use satellites and telescopes in space to learn more. Several satellites have been launched to study the Sun, including the Solar and Heliospheric **Observatory** (*SOHO*), launched in 1995, and the Solar Dynamics Observatory, launched in 2010.

However, there is still much we do not know about the Sun. If only we could get close enough to find out more!

The *SOHO* spacecraft is 1.5 million kilometres (nearly 1 million miles) closer to the Sun than Earth, but is still only one-hundredth of the distance to the Sun.

Once you've passed Mercury, things will start to get a lot hotter. The Sun is not all the same. It has several layers. The first thing you'll reach is the **corona** and it could be a bit of a shock.

## CROSSING THE CORONA

The corona is the outer atmosphere of the Sun but it's not a gentle introduction to our star. This glowing cloud of tiny gas **particles** begins as much as 1.6 million kilometres (1 million miles) from the surface of the Sun. You might think that it would be cooler, but the corona can be as hot as the centre of the Sun, with temperatures reaching millions of degrees.

The corona can only be seen from Earth when the bright disc of the Sun is covered by the Moon (see pages 32–33).

## CROSSING THE CHROMOSPHERE

If you could travel through the corona, things do cool down a bit. The inner atmosphere of the Sun is called the **chromosphere**, and its temperature is about 8,000 degrees Celsius (14,000 degrees Fahrenheit). The fiery chromosphere is shaken by violent explosions called solar flares.

You may see prominences soaring up from the chromosphere. These prominences are pillars of glowing super-heated gas. They can last for days. Eruptive prominences are most violent and can soar hundreds of thousands of kilometres into space.

A prominence erupts from the Sun's chromosphere at a temperature of more than 60,000 °C (108,000 °F).

### AMAZING FACTS

The Sun is mainly made of the gases hydrogen and **helium**. It contains 99 per cent of all the **matter** in the solar system.

The Sun spins round on its **axis,** just like Earth does. Unlike Earth, different parts of the Sun rotate at different speeds, because it is not solid.

## ON THE SURFACE

Beyond the chromosphere you would reach the surface of the Sun, also known as the **photosphere**. Although it's called the surface, you couldn't actually land there, even if it was cool enough. The Sun's surface is made of gases rather than the rocky crust of planets like Earth. The photosphere is where the heat and light that radiates out into the solar system comes from, and is the part of the Sun that can be seen from Earth.

New material is constantly rising to the surface from the Sun's core.

## WHAT DOES THE SURFACE LOOK LIKE?

When you get closer to the surface it appears to be covered in patches of different colours. These patches are caused by the streams of incredibly hot material rising up from the Sun's **core** to the relatively cool surface. Of course, at around 5,500 degrees Celsius (9,900 degrees Fahrenheit) it's not that cool. The photosphere will also feature darker patches called sunspots.

The Sun is much bigger than other objects in the solar system. Bigger or more massive objects have stronger forces of gravity. The gravity on the Sun's surface is 28 times that felt on Earth, so you would weigh 28 times as much. Humans can withstand this level of gravity, or g force, for a few seconds but any longer would result in death.

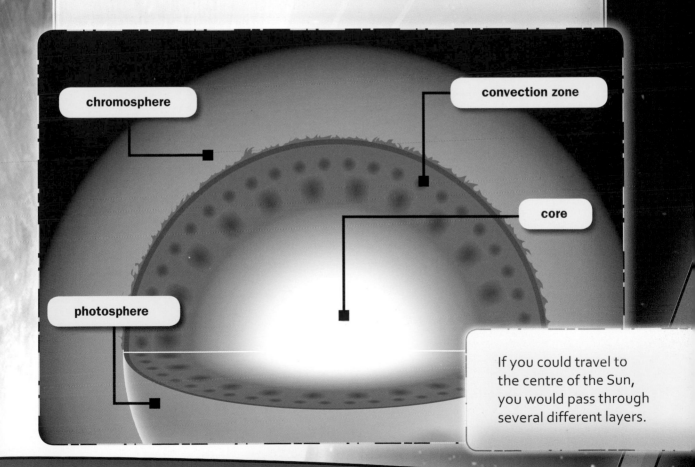

chromosphere

convection zone

core

photosphere

If you could travel to the centre of the Sun, you would pass through several different layers.

## TO THE CORE

The core of the Sun is where the action happens. At temperatures of around 15 million degrees Celsius (27 million degrees Fahrenheit), the Sun generates the energy that provides light and heat to Earth and all the other planets in the solar system. This light and heat takes hundreds of thousands of years to make their way from the core to the surface.

The Sun generates this energy by a process called **nuclear fusion**. **Atoms** are the tiny units that make up all matter. At incredibly high temperatures, the hydrogen atoms that make up most of the Sun can fuse, or join, together to make helium. When this happens, energy is released. When millions of tonnes of hydrogen atoms are fusing in the Sun every second, the amount of energy released is enormous.

## AMAZING FACTS

Controlled nuclear fusion could be a way to generate power on Earth. It releases huge amounts of energy but does not produce harmful waste like existing nuclear energy. The problem is that the fusion process needs very high temperatures, like those found at the core of the Sun.

The massive blast of a hydrogen bomb is created by an uncontrolled fusion reaction – a very small version of what happens inside the Sun.

## UNDER PRESSURE

The atoms are under huge pressure because of the size of the Sun. They are pressed together until they have a **density** 150 times greater than water. This means that if we could collect a teaspoon of matter from the Sun, it would have 150 times the **mass** of a teaspoon of water. Even if it was possible to find a material that could stand the heat of the core, it would be crushed by this enormous pressure.

# WHEN TO GO

There's an old joke that the best time to go to the Sun is at night. Of course, the Sun is always shining, even when we can't see it. There's not really a good time to go. The Sun is always incredibly hot, but the temperature on the surface is not always the same.

## SUNSPOTS

Since people first studied the Sun, they have noticed dark patches called sunspots appearing on the surface. These spots are cooler areas on the Sun's surface caused by disturbances inside the Sun. The good news for travellers is that they are cooler than the rest of the photosphere. The bad news is that they are still hot enough to melt any spacecraft.

### AMAZING FACTS

In previous centuries, astronomers thought that sunspots were so cool that people may be able to land on them. Sir William Herschel (1738–1822) suggested that they were openings in the Sun's atmosphere.

Sunspots are made up of a dark central area called the umbra, surrounded by a lighter area called the penumbra.

## SEASONS ON THE SUN

While sunspots may look small compared to the huge size of the Sun, many are bigger than Earth. They change size as they move across the photosphere. Samuel Heinrich Schwabe (1789–1875) was an amateur German astronomer. He observed that the number and size of sunspots followed a pattern that repeated itself about every 11 years. These patterns give the Sun "seasons". Although sunspots themselves are cooler, more heat reaches Earth from the Sun when there is greater sunspot activity.

## SOLAR FLARES

Solar flares are huge eruptions of gas from the Sun. Flares are most common at times of greatest sunspot activity and can reach temperatures of up to 100 million degrees Celsius (180 million degrees Fahrenheit). If you want to avoid encountering a solar flare, you should travel when there are fewer sunspots.

## WIND FROM THE SUN

Solar flares don't just affect the area around the Sun. Their impact is felt on Earth and across the solar system. The solar wind is a constant flow of radiation and atomic particles from the Sun out into the solar system. Solar flares throw out massive quantities of these particles, making the solar wind even stronger.

Astronomers are able to see amazing pictures of solar flares because of special space telescopes on satellites.

Earth's magnetic field and atmosphere protect us from the solar wind. However, the solar wind's effects can be seen in the Northern and Southern Lights (*Aurora borealis* and *Aurora australis*). These shimmering patterns of light appear close to the North and South Poles, at the northern and southern ends of Earth's axis.

## DON'T FORGET

You'll need to make sure your spacecraft has the right protection for your long journey in space, as you won't have Earth's atmosphere to shield you from the solar wind. Scientists are developing a magnetic shield that will protect spacecraft and astronauts from radiation in the solar wind.

The Northern and Southern Lights are the only signs of the solar wind that we can see from Earth.

## WHO'S WHO?

Richard Carrington (1826–1875) made a major contribution to our understanding of the Sun from his private observatory. He noted the connection between a huge solar flare and changes in the solar wind.

## LOOKING TO THE FUTURE

Maybe the best thing to do would be to wait until the Sun cools down before travelling there. As the hydrogen atoms join together to power the Sun, some of their mass is changed into energy. The Sun loses 4 million tonnes of its mass every second in the form of energy.

The Sun probably has enough fuel to last another 5 billion years. When its fuel starts to run out, the Sun will collapse in on itself due to the force of its gravity. This will cause it to become even hotter than before as the fusion reactions continue. Then, the reheated star will expand to become a red giant many times bigger than now.

Even Earth may be swallowed up by the expanding Sun in its red giant phase.

## WHITE DWARF

After millions of years, only a small white core, called a white dwarf, will be left behind. Over billions of years, the white dwarf will cool down. That might be a good time to visit. But, even if Earth has not been swallowed or burnt to a crisp by the dying Sun, humans would not be able to survive without its heat and light.

White dwarf stars fit a huge amount of mass into a very small space. This makes them have an extremely high density. If you could fill a 1-litre bottle with material from a white dwarf it would weigh about 1,000 tonnes!

**1**. Like other stars, the Sun began life inside a swirling cloud of gas and dust called a nebula. A clump of gas and dust formed, and grew larger and larger. Gravity pulled the material closer together.

**2**. The pressure and temperature at the centre of the clump grew. When it got hot enough, nuclear fusion reactions started. Energy was released into space and the Sun started to shine.

**3**. The new Sun burned brightly for millions of years. This is the stage our Sun is at now. As it gets older, its fuel will begin to run out and it will become less bright. A medium-sized star like our Sun shines for around 10 billion years. More massive stars use up their fuel more quickly, so they have shorter lives.

**6**. The white dwarf cools down and stops shining. It becomes a black dwarf and is almost invisible.

**5**. The material left behind will shrink to form a white dwarf. White dwarfs are about the size of a planet, but are very dense.

**4**. As the Sun's fuel runs out, the dying Sun will get bigger and become a red giant. Its outer layers of gas will start to escape into space.

Astronomers know about the likely future of the Sun from studying the fate of similar stars.

# WHO'S GOING WITH YOU?

You'll be lucky to find anyone to go with you on this mission to the Sun. Don't take any of your friends – a mission that involves certain doom will not make you popular with them. No one has ever been to the Sun so you won't be able to take a good guide.

## CREW MEMBER:

**GALILEO GALILEI (1564–1642)**
Galileo would be the first to volunteer for any mission to the Sun. He wasn't afraid to take risks when he proved the theory that the Earth goes round the Sun, against the wishes of the (Catholic) Church at the time. If he was alive today, he would probably be looking for new ways to find out about the Sun.

### POTENTIAL JOB:
engineer

## CREW MEMBER:

**NUCLEAR PHYSICIST**
Take someone who understands how nuclear fusion works – a nuclear physicist. Your journey could have real value if you can learn enough to help develop controlled nuclear fusion on Earth.

### POTENTIAL JOB:
scientific observer

## CREW MEMBER:
## ASTRONAUT

Great scientists are all very well but, on a journey like this, you'll need an experienced astronaut who knows what he or she is doing. It's a long way to the Sun, so you want a companion who's spent a long time in space, maybe working on the International Space Station.

### POTENTIAL JOB:
pilot

## CREW MEMBER:
## ALBERT EINSTEIN (1879–1955)

Einstein has probably done more to explain how physics works in space than anyone else. He developed theories about the behaviour of light and the impact of gravity on large bodies, such as stars. Although many of Einstein's ideas were based on theory, they have since been proved by experiments.

### POTENTIAL JOB:
navigator

# EARTHBOUND EXPLORERS

Even if it's impossible to visit the Sun, there is plenty you can find out without leaving Earth. One spectacle involving the Sun is rare but amazing.

## TOTAL ECLIPSE

While Earth is orbiting the Sun, the Moon orbits Earth. A solar eclipse happens when the Moon comes between Earth and the Sun in its orbit. The face of the Sun is partly or completely covered by the Moon. For the few seconds to a few minutes when the Sun's face is totally covered, the sky goes dark. This is a total eclipse. Then the Sun starts to become visible again.

shadow zone

Sun

Moon

observer sees total eclipse

This diagram shows how light from the Sun is blocked by the Moon during a total solar eclipse.

Total solar eclipses happen because the face of the Sun is 400 times larger than the Moon but is also 400 times further away, so the two look the same size.

A total eclipse only happens once every one or two years. You will be very lucky if you see one!

## DON'T FORGET

You should never look directly at the Sun during an eclipse, particularly through a device such as telescope or camera. But don't be scared away! To view the eclipse safely, make sure you have:

- a filter that is approved for viewing the Sun
- a way of projecting the eclipse on to a screen for viewing, for example by using a pinhole projector.

# INTERVIEW WITH AN ASTRONOMER

Dr Grace Wolf-Chase is an astronomer at the Adler Planetarium in Chicago, USA. She tries to discover how cold clouds of gas and dust collapse in space to form the different kinds of stars that we see in the sky.

**Q** *Why are you interested in the formation of stars?*

**A** I'm interested in how stars form because this tells us a lot about how our star, the Sun, and its planets (including Earth) formed. Understanding how different types of stars and planets form might tell us a lot about the conditions that lead to the development of life.

**Q** *What is the most interesting thing you have learned about stars?*

**A** It's that many of them have planets that orbit them just as the Earth orbits the Sun. When I was in school, we only knew about the planets in our Solar System. Since 1995, we have discovered over 680 planets orbiting other stars, and this number just keeps increasing. In fact, it's possible that most stars have planets. This means there may be a huge number of planets that are similar to Earth in the Universe!

**Q Do you think that there is life elsewhere in the Universe?**

**A** I think it's extremely likely, for two main reasons. Firstly, we've discovered that many stars have planets, and it seems likely that at least some of these planets have the right conditions for life to exist. Secondly, we've discovered that life on Earth is incredibly diverse. Many organisms can survive in environments that humans consider "extreme", such as very high or low temperatures or pressures. So it seems reasonable that there might be many environments in the Universe that are capable of supporting life.

**Q Which historical astronomer would you most like to meet and chat with?**

**A** There are many astronomers that haven't made it into the history books. I wish the names and lives of more women astronomers had been preserved through time! Because of this, I'd probably want to meet Caroline Herschel, since she is one of the few historical women astronomers whose life is well documented. She was born in 1750 and lived to the age of 98! She lived and worked with her brother, William, who was also an astronomer. Caroline discovered several comets and nebulae. She helped her brother to build telescopes and to develop a mathematical approach to astronomy.

# LIVING ON THE SUN?

The first and most obvious reason why we couldn't live on the Sun is the incredible heat. The highest temperature ever measured on Earth is 58 degrees Celsius (136 degrees Fahrenheit), whereas the temperature on the Sun varies from a few thousand to millions of degrees. Even in the coolest parts of the Sun's atmosphere, solid materials like metals would be turned to gas.

Even if we ignore the intense heat, the Sun is made up almost entirely of hydrogen and helium. One of the main reasons why we can live on Earth is because the atmosphere contains oxygen for living things to breathe. Oxygen combines with hydrogen to make water, which is also essential for living things.

## DON'T FORGET

Human beings and other animals need the following things to survive:

- Oxygen to breathe
- Water, which makes up about 60 per cent of the human body, and is needed to regulate body temperature and make the body function
- Food to give us energy.

None of these are found on the Sun and you'll need to take them with you when travelling in space.

Astronauts on the International Space Station have proved that people can stay in space for long periods, but they are only 386 kilometres (240 miles) from Earth.

## RADIATION RISK

The Sun does not just produce heat and light; the solar wind carries radiation and charged particles across the solar system. Earth's atmosphere protects us from this harmful radiation. The radiation can damage living cells, even at a distance of 150 million kilometres (93 million miles) from the Sun.

## LIVING WITHOUT THE SUN

Although we couldn't live on the Sun, we certainly couldn't live without it. The Sun is the source of nearly all the energy on Earth.

## NEITHER TOO NEAR, NOR TOO FAR

Earth is the right distance from the Sun so that water normally exists as a liquid on the surface. Earth is the only planet where this is the case. If we were any further from the Sun, our climate would be much colder, water would freeze, and we would not have the water we need to survive.

The Sun's warmth and light helps plants to grow and these feed humans and other animals. To understand how delicate this balance is, we only have to look at Earth's extremes. Very few things grow near the North and South Poles because the climate is too cold and dry. In deserts the climate is too hot and dry for many things to grow.

## NUMBER CRUNCHING

Other planets experience very extreme temperatures because they are nearer or further from the Sun. The average temperature on Mercury is 444 degrees Celsius (831 degrees Fahrenheit). On distant Neptune, it is a chilly −201 degrees Celsius (−330 degrees Fahrenheit).

The energy that these potato plants absorb from the Sun, transfers to us when we eat them.

## CHANGING CLIMATE

Scientists have shown that the actions of humans are changing this balance. Fumes from cars and industry are changing our atmosphere so that it is allowing less of the Sun's heat to escape. Our climate is becoming warmer, and many people believe that this could upset the balance of Earth's relationship with the Sun.

# MAP OF THE SOLAR SYSTEM

MERCURY

VENUS

EARTH

MARS

ASTEROID BELT

JUPITER

SATURN

URANUS

NEPTUNE

The sizes of the planets and their distances from the Sun are not to scale. To show all the planets' real distances from the Sun, this page would have to be about one kilometre long!

# TIMELINE

**Around 5 billion years ago**
Formation of the Sun and planets of the solar system.

**3000–1520 BC**
Stonehenge is built on Salisbury Plain in several stages.

**AD 1543**
Nicolaus Copernicus publishes the theory that Earth orbits around the Sun.

**1609**
Galileo makes his first observations with a telescope.

**1670s**
Cassini calculates the distance to the Sun.

**1687**
Isaac Newton publishes his theories of how gravity holds the planets in orbit around the Sun.

**1838**
Sir John Herschel conducts experiment to measure the Sun's energy.

**1843**
Samuel Heinrich Schwabe discovers that sunspots follow a pattern or cycle every 11 years.

**1859**
Richard Carrington observes a solar flare for the first time.

**1959**
*Luna 1* spacecraft detects solar wind.

**1961**
First manned spaceflight by astronaut Yuri Gagarin.

**1962–1975**
NASA launches a series of Orbiting Solar Observatories to study the Sun.

**1995**
*SOHO* probe is launched into orbit around the Sun.

**2010**
Solar Dynamics Observatory (SDO) is launched. It observes the Sun every 10–50 seconds to see small changes that previous probes could not capture.

# FACT FILE

**POSITION:**

Outer region of the Milky Way galaxy

**DISTANCE FROM EARTH:**

150 million kilometres (93 million miles). Light from the Sun takes about 8 minutes to reach Earth

**SIZE:**

1,392,000 kilometres (866,000 miles) in diameter

**MASS:**

330,000 times greater than the mass of Earth

**TEMPERATURE:**

- Surface: 5,500 degrees Celsius
          (9,900 degrees Fahrenheit)
- Core: 15 million degrees Celsius
          (27 million degrees Fahrenheit)

**MADE FROM:**

- Hydrogen: 71%
- Helium: 27%
- Other gases: 2%

**SATELLITES:**

Eight planets orbit around the Sun (Mercury, Venus, Earth, Mars, Jupiter, Saturn, Uranus, Neptune), plus at least three dwarf planets and many other asteroids and comets

# GLOSSARY

**atmosphere** layer of gases surrounding a planet

**atom** smallest unit of matter. Everything is made up of atoms.

**axis** imaginary line around which something rotates, such as a planet

**chromosphere** inner part of the Sun's atmosphere, above the visible surface

**core** centre of the Sun

**corona** outer part of the Sun's atmosphere

**crewed** worked on and operated by people, for example on a train, boat, or spaceship

**density** amount of matter, or mass, contained within a particular volume

**diameter** width of a circle at its widest point

**dwarf planet** object that orbits the Sun but is smaller than the eight recognized planets, such as Pluto

**energy** the capacity to do work – for example heat energy from the Sun warms Earth

**gas** matter, such as oxygen, that is able to expand without limit unless it is contained

**gravity** force that pulls objects towards each other. Big objects, such as planets, have much stronger gravity than smaller objects, such as people.

**helium** gas lighter than air, formed when two hydrogen atoms fuse in the core of the Sun

**hydrogen** lightest and most abundant element in the solar system, which makes up most of the Sun

**mass** amount of material that makes up an object

**matter** anything that has mass and fills space, including solids, liquids, and gases

**navigate** find the way, particularly when at sea or in the air

**nuclear fusion** process in which hydrogen atoms join together to make new atoms

**observatory** building with telescopes and other instruments for observing (looking at) stars and planets

**orbit** path of an object around a star or planet

**oxygen** gas present in Earth's atmosphere that most living things need to breathe

**particle** tiny part, such as part of an atom

**photosphere** surface of the Sun, normally visible from Earth

**probe** unmanned spacecraft designed to send back data and images of space

**radiation** tiny particles, smaller than an atom, emitted (thrown out) by the Sun

**satellite** object, often human-made, that orbits a larger object

**solar flare** sudden and violent release of matter and energy from the Sun

**solar system** the Sun, the planets, and other objects that are in orbit around it

**sunspot** darker area on the surface of the Sun

**telescope** instrument that makes distant objects look bigger

# FIND OUT MORE

## BOOKS

*Astronauts (Graphic Careers)*, David West (Franklin
   Watts, 2010)

*Space: A Children's Encyclopedia* (Dorling Kindersley, 2010)

*The Sun (The Earth and Space)*, Steve Parker
   (Wayland, 2009)

*Will the Sun Ever Burn Out? Earth, Sun, and Moon*,
   Rosalind Mist (Heinemann Library, 2007)

## WEBSITES

www.bbc.co.uk/newsround/14126818
or www.bbc.co.uk/science/space/solarsystem
Find out more about the solar system on the BBC's website.

www.hubblesite.org
Find images of the solar system and beyond from the
Hubble Space Telescope.

www.nasa.gov/audience/forkids/kidsclub/flash/index.html
NASA is the US space agency. NASA's Kids Club website
features loads of space news, games, and fun activities.

## PLACES TO VISIT

**Royal Observatory Greenwich**
Blackheath Avenue, Greenwich, London SE10 8XJ
www.nmm.ac.uk/visit/planetarium-shows

**The National Space Centre**
Exploration Drive, Leicester LE4 5NS
www.spacecentre.co.uk

## SIGHTS TO SEE

If you get the chance, you should try to see a solar eclipse. These happen rarely and can only be seen from certain places. Other Sun-related sights you might be able to see include the *Aurorae*, which appear in the extreme north and south of our planet.

## FURTHER RESEARCH

- Stars: The Sun is just one of billions of stars in the Universe. There is plenty you can find out about other stars and amazing things like supernovas and black holes.
- Scientists: People like Galileo and Newton made amazing discoveries that helped us understand more about the Sun. You can find out more about their lives and discoveries and the many other advances of the Scientific Revolution.
- Effects of the Sun on Earth: Research the different ways that Earth's relationship with the Sun affects people and living things, from seasons and energy to how we measure time.

## WARNING

Make sure that you never look directly at the Sun. Although you can look at stars through binoculars or a telescope, you must never use these to look at the Sun. Looking at the Sun can damage your eyes.

# INDEX